Frontispiece: Church by the Pond (see page 48 for further details)

Contemporary
BOHEMIAN
LACE

VĚRA LEVÁ-ŠKROVÁNOVÁ
Edited by STAN SKOUMAL

DRYAD PRESS LTD London

ISBN 0 8521 9735 7

Typeset by Servis Filmsetting Ltd, Manchester
and printed in Great Britain by
R. J. Acford
Chichester
Sussex
for the publishers
Dryad Press Ltd
8 Cavendish Square
London W1M 0AJ

CONTENTS

INTRODUCTION

In the second half of the last century Bohemia was one of the principal workshops producing lace for the rich of Europe. Over 30,000 lacemakers are known to have worked in their homes across the country and more were working in adjoining Maravia and Slovakia, the lands which together with Bohemia were to form Czechoslovakia at the end of the First World War. The unique achievements of contemporary Bohemian and Slovak lace should be seen against this background.

Despite its dominance during that period, this aspect of the lace's history is little known since at the height of its fame it was not sold under its own name. The industry, and an industry it indeed was, was then controlled from Vienna, the capital of the Austro-Hungarian empire of which Bohemia, Moravia and Slovakia were then parts, by a company owned by the Austrian imperial family which was commissioning lace from Bohemian lacemakers to export them worldwide under the label of Viennese lace.

The lace made for the imperial venture had to meet the demands of fashion of the time which was for Brussels-style lace and it was this type of lace the lacemakers were asked to produce from patterns supplied by Vienna in preference to their own traditional designs. In time these alien patterns began to merge with the traditional ones to become 'Viennese lace', which brought Bohemian lace to the notice of the world, albeit anonymously.

It is not clearly established when lacemaking began to be practised in Central Europe. The earliest evidence of lace in Bohemia comes from a number of fourteenth-century paintings which show lace attached to the clothing of persons in the picture. Neither is it known with certainty where the craft came from, but it is believed that it was from Italy, though by an indirect route through Dalmatia via Raguse (Dubrovnik) which was then a major political and cultural centre competing for power with Venice. It was also a leading centre of lacemaking. The first reliable evidence of lacemaking in Bohemia comes from the second half of the sixteenth century and refers to a flourishing export trade in lace made in the mountain regions of western Bohemia.

The next milestone in the history of Bohemian lace was reached under the tutelage of a Flemish lacemaker, Magdalen Gramb from Malines. She came to

Bohemia with her German husband to take over the lands of a Czech nobleman executed by the Catholic Habsburgs after their final victory over the Protestant Czechs in 1620. These lands were around the small town of Vamberk on the Bohemian/Moravian borders. The new lady of the manor, soon after settling on the estate, set out to teach lacemaking to women of working families in the villages belonging to her husband. She was so successful in her endeavour that one hundred years later in the middle of the eighteenth century some 20,000 lacemakers were known to work around Vamberk.

From that time on Bohemian lacemaking was riding the crest of a wave and over the following hundred years a number of lacemaking schools were set up in Bohemia, culminating in the establishment of the Royal School of Lacemaking in Prague in 1867 and the Bohemian School of Lacemaking in Vamberk in 1889. The latter then finally established Vamberk as the principal lacemaking area in the land.

The opening of the Royal School was followed 12 years later in Prague by the lace exporting venture of the Austrian imperial family which brought Bohemian lacemaking to the next high point of its history, even though only anonymously and for only a brief period. Soon afterwards in the face of devastating competition from machine-made lace, the decline of traditional lacemaking began.

In Bohemia, unlike in many other centres, the decline did not spell the death of professional lace. By coincidence it occurred when, at the beginning of twentieth century, powerful intellectual forces threw the artistic world into a search for new forms and new media through which to express foreboding of the full impact of industrial revolution and found lace technique a suitable new tool. In the countries in the vanguard of the new movement such as France, Germany and particularly Central Europe, some artists quickly developed an extraordinary feeling for their new medium, now freed from its purely decorative character, and learned to communicate through threads and knots artistic expressions with the same virtuosity as painters with strokes of a brush and composers with a sequence of tones. In their hands lace was reborn.

The overlap of the abrupt decline of traditional lace and the equally abrupt rise of lace as a medium of fine art tends to conceal the fact that traditional lace and artlace are essentially two different objects. While both require an artist to create the design and a craftsman to realise it, there is a difference in the objective of design which sets them apart. In the case of traditional lace the designer's aim is to create a decorative object for a well-defined application, while an artist freed from this restriction will design lace with an intellectual purpose which then stands as a creation in its own right. To differentiate between these two forms of lace two new terms came to be used. Namely that of *applied lace* for the former and that of *expressive lace* for the latter. In the last ten years a third concept gained currency, that of *monumental lace* which refers to creations made with threads and knots of various traditional and high technology fibres on a scale to be used by architects and designers of large interiors.

As the fortunes of applied lace declined almost to the point of extinction in the world, in Czechoslovakia vestiges of lacemaking have been preserved in government-funded rural centres where small groups (three or four) of craftswomen are employed as full-time lacemakers to produce traditional and modern applied lace for a variety of handmade textile items. These centres have become focal points of current lacemaking, where lace working artists associate with lacemakers to design and to make applied lace for the trade and expressive lace as works of art.

On the whole the centres have been a success, linking contemporary lace with its past but they have failed in one respect. It was originally hoped that the work of the centres would arrest the decline of lace as an industry and even perhaps reverse it, but this has not happened. Fewer young people are coming forward to seek a living in lacemaking and it seems that eventually traditional lacemaking will survive only as a hobby among enthusiasts as has happened elsewhere. It is however another matter where expressive lace is concerned. The reputation of Bohemian and Slovak expressive lace is riding high both at home and in the world at large, probably higher than was the fame of Bohemian lace 100 years ago. There is little doubt that as an artistic medium, lace has an assured future in Czechoslovakia on a full professional footing.

The present status of expressive lace in Czechoslovakia may have some connection with the role lacemaking historically played in the culture of the nation. However, more than anything, expressive lace owes its fame to a trio of single-minded artists and teachers of unique talents, vision and determination who on the formation of Czechoslovakia in 1918 set the textile department of the College of Fine and Applied Arts in Prague on a new road of creativity. In their lifetime they brought up a generation of artists capable of continuing and developing the work. The trio was Professor Emily Paličková, Professor Antonín Kybal and Professor Marie Vaňková-Kuchyňková. Their pioneering work in developing the concept of expressive lace and establishing it as an artistic discipline earned them a place among the giants of contemporary Czechoslovak art.

Reference to the pioneers of contemporary Czechoslovak artlace would not be complete without a mention of Elena Holéczy, whose contribution to the development of expressive lace in Slovakia was comparable to the work of the Prague trio, though against a different background. Slovakia, although like Bohemia and Moravia also a part of the old Austro-Hungarian monarchy, was exposed more to the influence of Hungary than of Austria and Slovak lacemaking missed the great boom that Bohemian lace enjoyed in the last century. Therefore it remained uninfluenced by the demands of Western fashion, staying more conservative in outlook, and Holéczy's work had to start on a different plane than that of her Prague counterparts.

The key to the appreciation of contemporary expressive lace is to understand that in this concept lace is only the means to an end and not an end in itself as is the case with applied lace. In essence, expressive lace is a drawing, but a drawing made with threads and knots through which the artist realises an intellectual input instead of using drawing tools or paints. As in the case of a more traditional artist who chooses between pen and pencil, between paper and canvas or between palete knife and brush to obtain the wanted effect, so must the lace artist choose from many available materials, decide on the type of stitches and judge the effect of various techniques to ensure that the end product is what she wants. Perhaps the only point on which a painter and a designer of expressive lace differ is that expressive lace itself is not always actually made by the designer but often left to a lacemaker to do.

Clearly, expressive lace belongs in the world of arts with some artists specialising in it as others specialise in wood, glass, collages and other media. It is an absorbing medium and most of its artists do not work in any other field, or if they do then they usually restrict their work to related fields such as weaving, yardage printing or other textile applications. Not surprisingly all contemporary lace working artists are women.

Věra Levá-Škrovánová whose work is presented in this book studied under Professor Paličková between 1949 and 1953 at the College of Fine and Applied Arts in Prague (an autonomous school of Prague University) and has remained associated with expressive lace ever since. Unlike most of her colleagues she is not a single medium artist. Having qualified from the Prague School of Graphic Design under Professor Dillinger before transferring to art lace under Professor Paličková, her other major artistic interest is book illustrations, particularly illustrations for technical and scientific literature.

Under both of her teachers drawing was the backbone of Věra Levá-Škrovánová's interest and it remains the backbone of her work. All her laces start as drawings and the design of the ensuing lace is dominated entirely by it. The lace is ruthlessly made to comply with it. No allowances are made for the technical considerations of lacework and indeed relatively coarse materials are used purposely to detract from the finesse of lace and to emphasise the contents of the picture. But at the same time Věra Levá-Škrovánová uses lace with subtle mastery with which she guides the spectator's eye to the central point of the picture by notions of light and shade created by control of her stitches.

The laces pictured in this book are a short selection from her vast freelance work. Most of them reflect her childhood experiences in rural Bohemia and her years as an art student in Prague. Her mother-and-child pictures are the madonnas which fascinated her in the paintings over which she marvelled in village churches, her dancing figures are her fellow students at the festive gatherings of her student years and the musicians are people who created an atmosphere of youthful joy.

However, there is another side to Věra Levá-Škrovánová which shows in her work commissioned by architects, public bodies and local authorities. Such commissions are an important source of income to artists in Czechoslovakia. In this work, which often involves designs stretching over tens of feet, her designs remain disciplined to the point of severity to meet the commissioned purpose, sometimes with realism and at other times by detached abstractions.

When designing her laces Věra Levá-Škrovánová begins with sketches either inspired by daily events or conceived as studies with deliberate orientation for commissioned work. The purpose is to capture at first an idea in a visual form and no consideration is given at this stage to the ultimate form of the lace picture. When an idea eventually reaches paper, several versions are drawn to see the subject in broad context and each is roughly sketched as a lace. Materials, colours and the construction of the lace are now considered. The criterion of final choice is how well a particular lace is likely to embody the artistic side of the design as depicted in the drawing.

The final stage starts with a full-size or a scale drawing of the chosen alternative. This is then segmented into areas for different stitches. The choice of stitches follows and starts with first pinning out the areas where cloth-stitch will be needed and then designating areas best suited for the use of tape. The kind of tape and the way the tapes will be shaped are decided next. This done, fillings are considered for the remaining parts of the drawing which are chosen to highlight the essential points of the picture. Finally leafwork is assigned to small incidental areas and areas of unavoidable detail. The lace, as it appears at the end of the design process, can be characterised as of an almost austere simplicity achieved largely through the boldness of approach and omissions of detail. With few areas of clothstitch, one or two tapes, little filling and small pieces of leafwork here and there Věra Levá-Škrovánová can and does create pictures radiating movement, atmosphere and artistic grace.

In the pages which follow only a fraction of Věra Levá-Škrovánová's output is presented. While it would be rash to describe her as a typical Czechoslovak artist in her field, her work can be regarded as a representative sample of the work currently done in the country and as an example of an extraordinary feel for the medium which contemporary Bohemian and Slovak artists working with expressive lace possess.

1. Adam and Eve

An example of the versatility of braid or tape lace in an amusing interpretation of a classical theme. Snake is a single length with overlapping.

12

2. Morning Grooming

Three well-designed tapes together with masterly omissions of detail, a characteristic of Věra Levá-Škrovánová's work, make the complete picture.

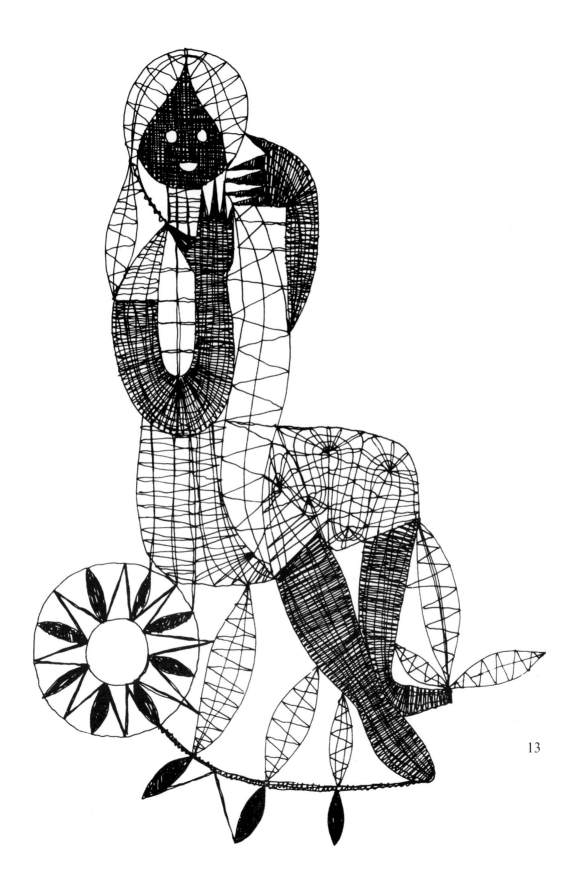

13

3. Our Skoda, Model 1897

The complexity of shapes and stitches in the design of the figures is contrasted by the simplicity of the car tapes and half-stitch filling. Extraneous placing of the bird gives excellent balance to this piece.

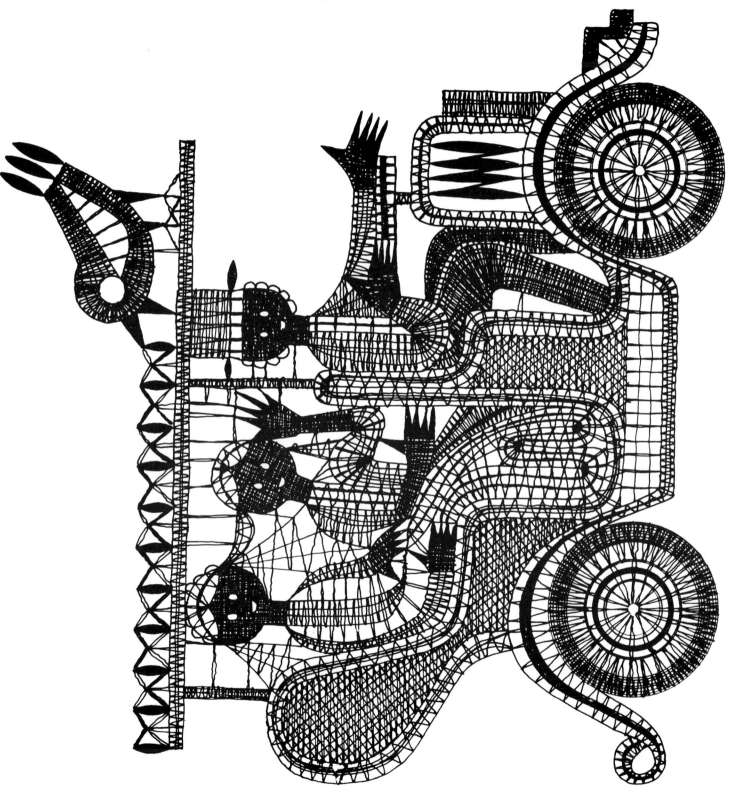

4. Pied Piper

A difficult lace to make, requiring either frequent interruptions of tapes or overlapping. A well-conceived design with the rats providing an essential horizontal element to balance the otherwise overwhelmingly vertical character.

5. Tree by the Lake

An example of a lace where multi-tape realisation of a design was chosen by the artist in preference to the use of a single strip of lace to preserve the artistic content of the original drawing.

16

6. An Argument

Traditional folklore motif translated into lace. Remarkable for its symmetry and the birds cleverly formed by single tapes.

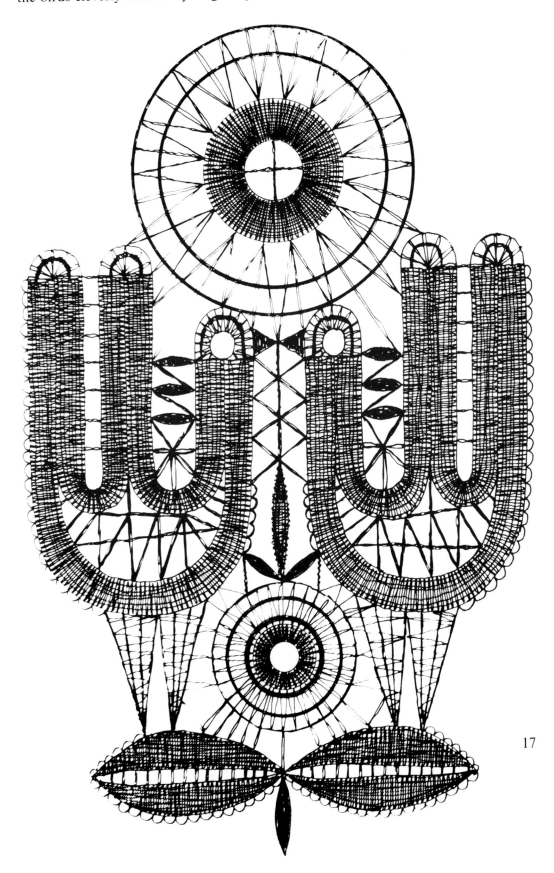

17

7. Peasant with a Flower

A remarkable harmony of the arm/flower and the hip curves. The weavers from the upper cloth-stitch leaves are taken through to the lower leaves.

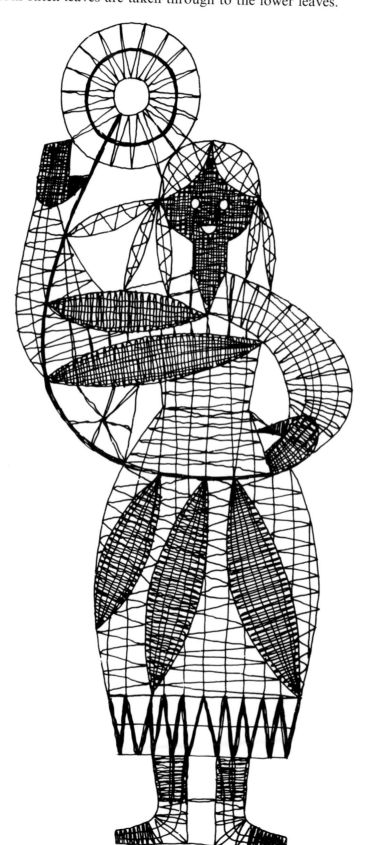

18

8. Rocking Horse

The horse, movement and the circle amount to a rocking horse. The head and body of the horse are formed by a single tape.

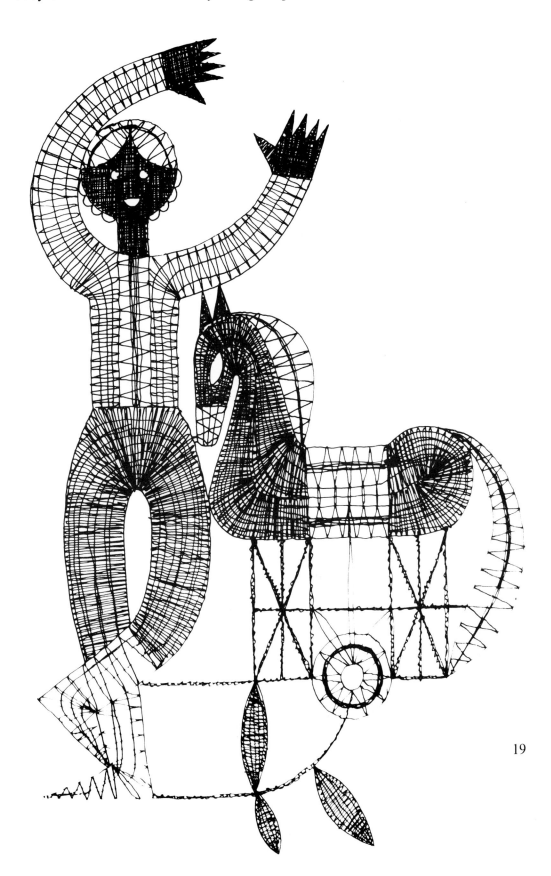

19

9. Boy with his Horse

A likeness achieved by remarkably simple means. The horse's right hind leg is a separate tape derived from the cloth-stitch area to avoid complications with too many pairs.

10. With Flowers and Song

A simple design but demanding considerable skill to cope with the amount and placing of half-stitch in the lace. The piper's right arm is omitted without loss of realism.

11. Two songbirds

Feeling of *joie de vivre* radiates from this very simple design. Note the use of a single tape to make both arms.

12. Flute and Charm

A clever way of forming the shape of the female body and of achieving the three-dimensional effect of the legs by lace strips.

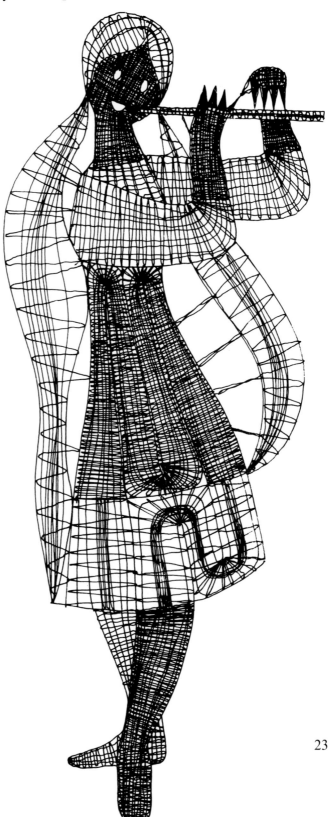

23

13. I am a Musician!

One of the simplest laces in the collection made mostly with twisted and untwisted pairs. A village band musician who knows his worth.

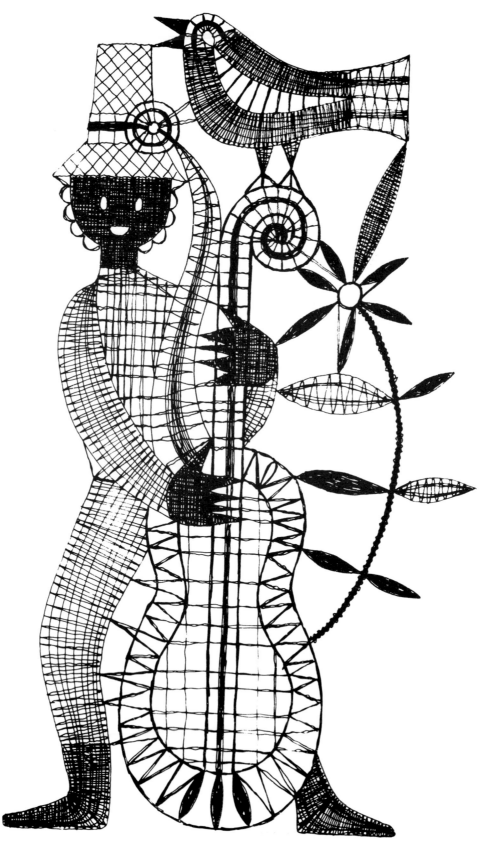

24

14. Playing Jazz

An example of the perfect balance between artistic and structural considerations of a design. The artist in Věra Levá created the movement and the music in the design while Věra Levá, the technical illustrator, constructed the lace.

15. Village Band

Again Věra Levá as artist and Věra Levá as a technician at work. The artist masterly portraying a band of different but equally strong characters and the technician achieving a perfectly constructed lace.

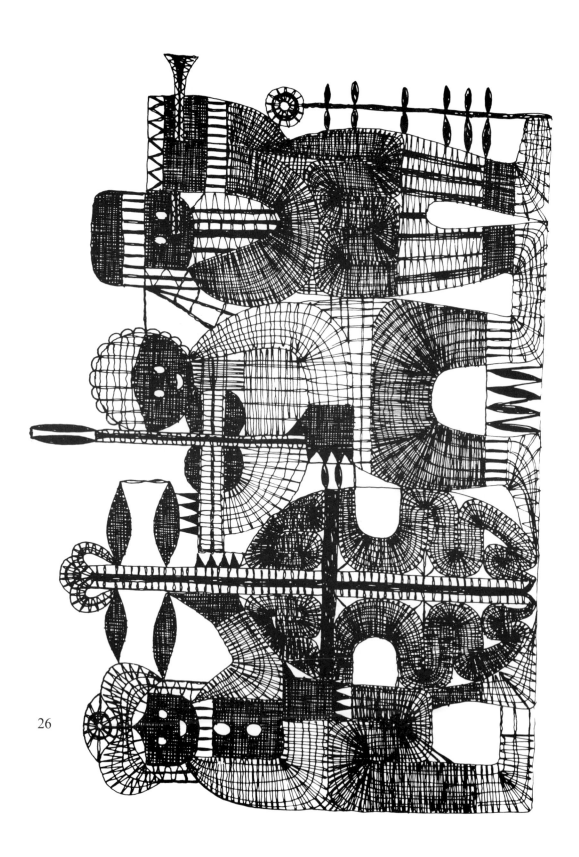

26

16. Double Bass

Detail from the previous design. Note the redesigned left leg which now is a tape extended from the leafwork of the fingers of the right hand.

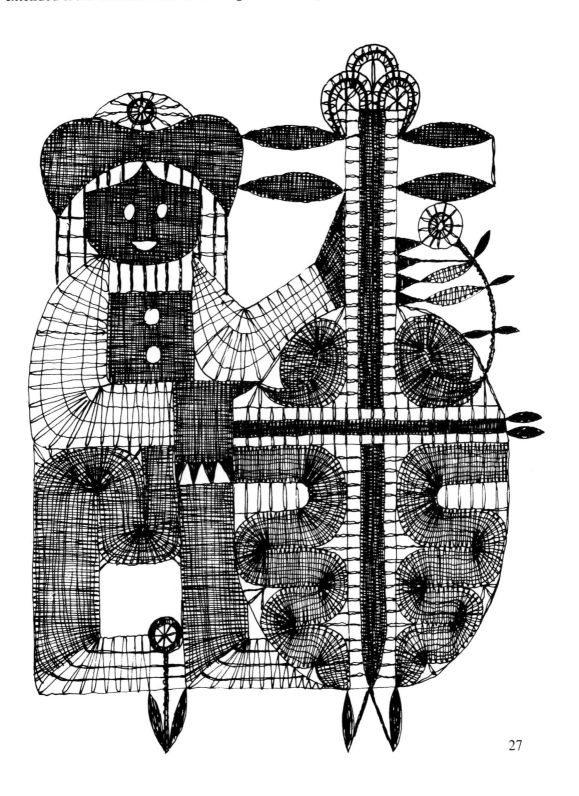

17. Listening to a Fiddler

One of the more complex designs with each tape being a masterpiece. The sense of music and movement is overwhelming.

28

18. Singing with a Fiddler

Movement beautifully captured by the postures. Note the identical way both figures are made; reduction of pairs below faces and single tapes forming lower parts of the bodies.

29

19. Two with Pipes (and a child)

An ingenious way of showing long hair and a bearded face. The smoothly flowing curves of the child's body underscore the sensation of movement.

30

20 Musical Pair

The U-shaped lace forming the trousers gives them an air of elegance and there is an air of movement to the shape of the skirt. The lower tape of the skirt runs through the left leg and both feet, ending in the flower.

21. Two Listeners

The two bottom leaves of the branch held by the child are parts of the tapes forming the skirt.

22. Madonna with Child

An abstracted design emphasising the child by elimination of detail in the mother's body. The mother's hand is retained to stress the child's safety in the embrace. An all-tape lace including the flower springing from child's left foot.

23. Madonna with Child and Flowers

Another approach to the subject in the previous plate. (Symbolism in the child's face should not be mistaken with the symbolism in the face of the musician in Design 19!)

34

24. Isn't he a Lovely Baby!

Most ingeniously the mother's skirt, together with the three horizontal leaves, is formed by a single tape starting in the left upper leaf and ending in the right hand end of the lower leaf. The child is also formed from a single lace strip.

35

25. He's Lovely and he's Mine

A less prominent position of the child than in the previous work brings the mother to share the focus of the design. Pairs of the leafwork in the fringe of the skirt extend to make the mother's legs.

26. First Steps

In this design the choice of body textures indicates the equality of both figures in the picture. Seven tapes make this complicated lace.

27. Mother, Child and Admirer

Two interesting tapes in this design run one from the head of the child to the head of the bird and the other from the top leaf of the plant through the body of the bird to its tail.

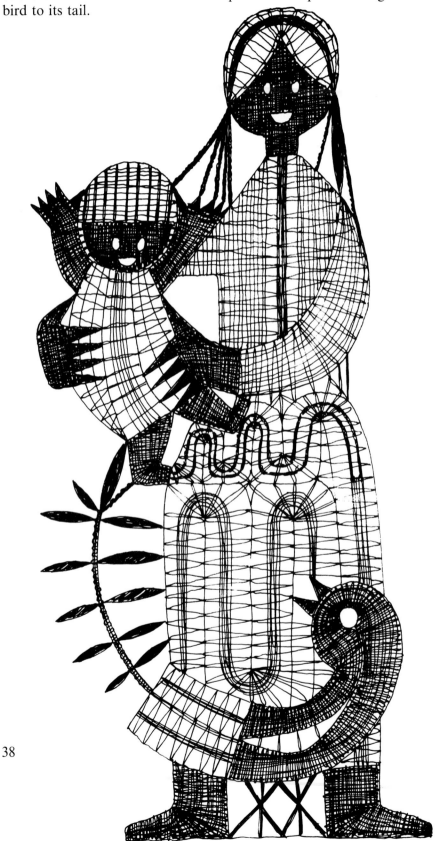

38

28. Happy Family

A design based on an intriguing central strip which makes the child's arms and hands, and the faces of both parents, all in one piece.

29. Family Celebration

Again a single lace strip supports the family motif, starting with father's hand and running through the central flower to end in the flower on the mother's side.

40

30. Head Motif – First Lace

Together with the following three plates this design is part of a set showing the transition from an ornate concept of the theme into a relatively simple one.

31. Head Motif – Second Lace

A secondary theme, a single tape bird, replaces some of the more flamboyant filling.

42

32. Head Motif – Third Lace

The head is now reduced to a piece of cloth plus tape which extends into the flower and plant. The bird now becomes the more complex part of the design.

43

33. Head Motif – Fourth Lace

The ultimate reduction to two very simple tapes and a piece of multi-pair lace still preserves the artistic content of the motif.

44

34. Portrait I

A striking design of hair obtained by a single tape.

35. Portrait II

A variant of the previous lace but here the hair is made with two tapes; one tape starts in the centre of the flower and broadens as it becomes part of the hair, while the other fills the rest of the hair area.

36. Cathedral by the Bridge

A design executed by frequent removal and addition of pairs. The relative austerity of the buildings is softened by incorporation of the tree with birds made with tapes and a variety of filling.

37. Church by the Pond

The concept is again dominated by multi-pair lace as in the previous design. Swans and fish are neatly incorporated in the water wave tapes.

38. An Outing on the Bridge

Brilliant use of tapes in a conceptually homogeneous but complex design.

49

39. First Dancing Pair

This design and the four which follow are sketches of Czech folklore dancing. The dancers are pictured in Czech national costumes. The skirt here is a single tape.

50

40. Second Dancing Pair

The skirt is again a single strip but this time the tape incorporates all three legs below it starting with the girl's right toe and ending in the man's leg.

51

41. Third Dancing Pair

The dancers are dancing 'dupak', a dance characterised by stamping the floor. An additional tape is used in the skirt to compensate for the extension of the main tape into the girl's right leg.

42. Fourth Dancing Pair

The skirt is now part of the tape extending from the girl's left hand. Most of her partner's body is another single tape.

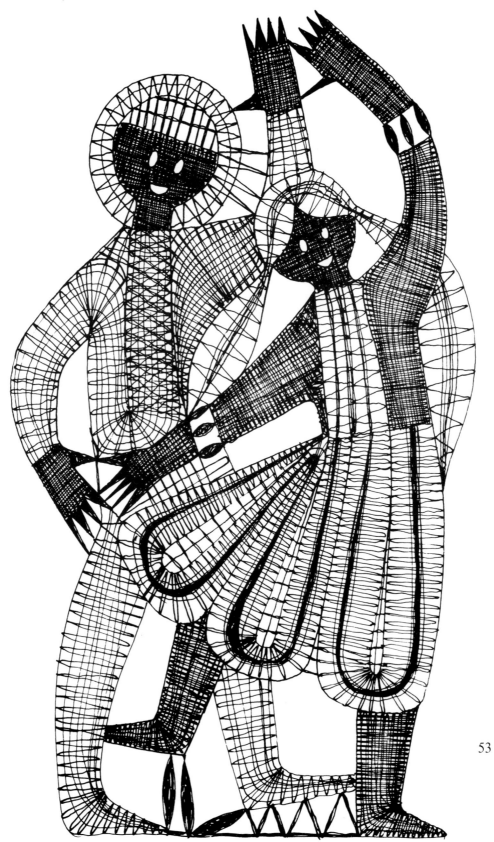

53

43. Fifth Dancing Pair

Two tapes make the skirt and apron combination here. The skirt tape starts at the circular sleeve and the apron tape derives from it at the boy's small finger running to the girl's right toe.

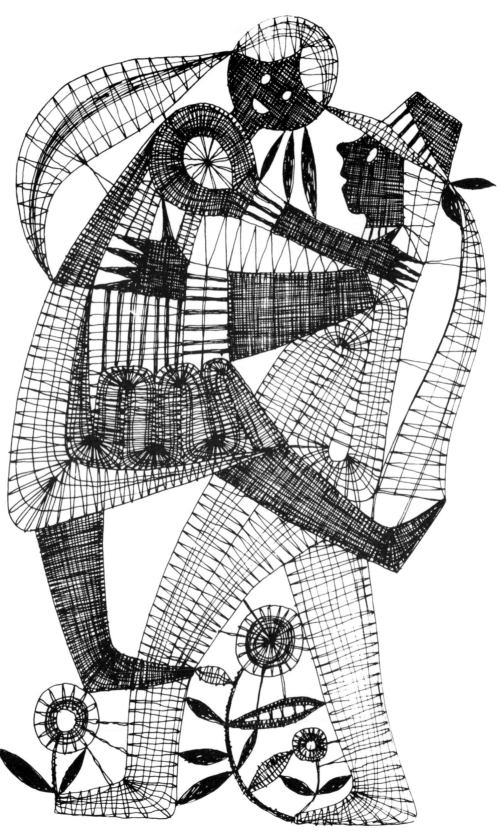

44. Children's Games

Two contrasting approaches to the use of tapes in the design of dancing figures. Both arms and legs are hung on.

45. Spring Joy

Another case of two-tape work. The left arms are again hung on. The flower attached to the dancers symbolises the seasonal connection.

46. Three Sisters
The skilful use of faces and arms to obtain a well-rounded lace.

47. Meet My Two Sisters

Delightfully simple interpretation of the three-face motif by three tapes. The lighter density of legs of the central figure helps to create a three-dimensional effect.

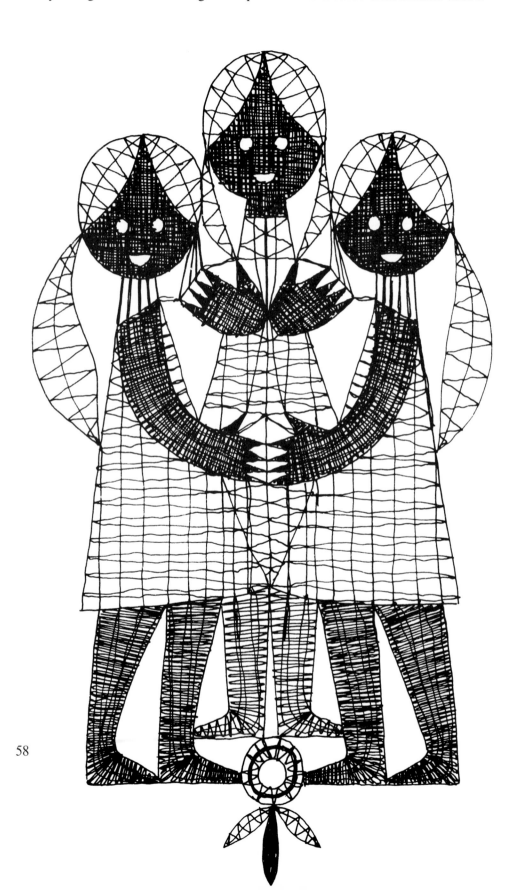

48. Three More Sisters

Very original design combining simplicity of lace with economy of space.

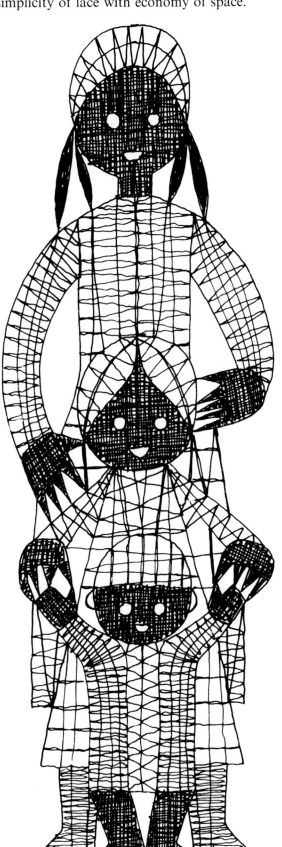

59

49. A Greeting to Father

Another example of an effective design obtained by omission of detail and an inventive combination of tapes.

60

50. Flowerpot

Věra Levá's doodle made of seven tapes and leafwork.

FURTHER READING

Clare, Raie, *The Dryad Book of Bobbin Lace*, Dryad Press
Dye, Gilian, *Beginning Bobbin Lace*, Dryad Press
Dye, Gilian, *Bobbin Lace Braid*, B T Batsford
Fisher, Jennifer, *Braid Lace for Today*, Dryad Press
Fisher, Jennifer, *Torchon Lace for Today*, Dryad Press
Hains, Valerie, *The Lavendon Collection of Bobbin Lace Patterns*, Dryad Press
Nottingham, Pamela, *Bobbin Lacemaking*, B T Batsford
Stillwell, Alexandra, *Drafting Torchon Lace Patterns*, Dryad Press
Sutton, Edna, *Bruges Flower Lace*, Dryad Press
Voysey, Cynthia, *Bobbin Lace in Photographs*, B T Batsford
Withers, Jean, *Mounting and Using Lace*, Dryad Press

Suppliers

Frank Herring and Sons
27 High West Street
Dorchester
DT1 1UP

Honiton Lace Shop
44 High Street
Honiton
Devon

D J Hornsby
149 High Street
Burton Latimer
Kettering
Northants

Capt J R Howell
19 Summerwood Lane
Halsall
Nr Ormskirk
Lancs
L39 8RG

Sebalace
76 Main Street
Addingham
Ilkley
West Yorks
LS29 0PL

T Brown
Woodside
Greenlands Lane
Prestwood
Great Missenden
Bucks

A. Sells
49 Pedley Lane
Clifton
Shelford
Beds

C & D Springett
21 Hillmorton Road
Rugby
Warwicks
CV22 5BE

Enid Taylor
Valley House Craft Studio
Ruston
Scarborough
North Yorks
YO13 9QE

George White
Delaheys Cottage
Thistle Hill
Knavesborough
North Yorks

English Lace School
Honiton Court
Rockbeare
Nr Exeter
Devon

Mace and Nairn
89 Crane Street
Salisbury
Wilts

The Lace Guild
c/o The Hollies
53 Audnam
Stourbridge
West Midlands
DY8 4AE

D H Shaw
47 Zamor Crescent
Thurscroft
Rotherham
South Yorks

John and Jennifer Ford
5 Squirrels Hollow
Boney Way
Walsall

Shireburn Lace
Finkle Court
Finkle
Sherburn in Elmet
North Yorks

Newham Lace Equipment
15 Marlow Close
Basingstoke
Hants

B Phillips
Pantglas
Cellan
Lampeter
Dyfed